W0081635

Cello Time Duets

30 progressive duets for cello

Kathy and David Blackwell

Welcome to **Cello Time Duets**. You'll find:

- duets using 1st position, including backward and forward extensions, to pieces using 4th position, plus 2nd and 3rd positions
- some duets with parts of equal difficulty and some with a harder part suitable for a teacher or more advanced student
- an additional six mini duet warm-ups exploring different techniques and skills
- a variety of musical styles, from classical and folk repertoire to original compositions
- material suitable for both sight-reading and concert performance
- an ideal resource to help develop ensemble skills
- the perfect companion to the books in the *Cello Time* series
- a book just for cello players—this collection is not compatible with *Fiddle Time Duets* or *Viola Time Duets*.

OXFORD
UNIVERSITY PRESS

Great Clarendon Street, Oxford OX2 6DP, England.

Impression: 1

ISBN 978–0–19–357419–9

Music and text origination by Julia Bovee
Printed in Great Britain

Welcome to **Cello Time Duets**.

Here you'll find 30 attractive and progressive cello duets to enjoy, from arrangements of classical and folk music to imaginative original compositions. There are also six mini duet warm-ups that explore different techniques and skills.

The duets in each section correspond approximately to the technical levels of the books in the *Cello Time* series: *Starters, Joggers, Runners, Sprinters*, and *Solo Time for Cello Book 1*. **Cello Time Duets** is thus an invaluable resource for students at various stages of learning, from an established beginner (approx. Initial/Grade 1) to Grade 4–5 level. Some duets have parts of equal difficulty, while some have a harder part (usually the lower) suitable for a teacher or more advanced student, making it a useful resource for students at different stages of learning to play together.

The book also provides ideal sight-reading material and great repertoire for concert performance. You'll find a range of keys, styles, techniques, and much opportunity to develop ensemble skills in this attractive collection. A range of free resources, including some additional duet material, is free to download at www.kathyanddavidblackwell.co.uk

So find a duet partner and enjoy exploring the diverse range of music in **Cello Time Duets**!

Kathy and David Blackwell

Contents

Mini Duet Warm-ups   4

Starting
1. Let's Celebrate!   6
2. Bird Song   7
3. Run for your life!   8
4. Bill Grogan's Goat   9
5. Lani sem kupil   10

Jogging
6. Silver Moon Boat   11
7. Buttered Peas   12
8. Sharing a Surprise! (Haydn)   13
9. Lullaby for Angus   14
10. Two Trick Pony   15
11. Sort of Rocky   16

Running
12. Eh soom boo kawaya   17
13. Morag's Cradle Song   18
14. Melody (Beethoven)   19
15. Rondeau (Saint-Georges)   20
16. March (Handel)   21
17. Simple Gifts (Brackett)   22
18. One, two, three, four, paper hat   23

Sprinting
19. Dance (Beethoven)   24
20. La Mourisque (Susato)   25
21. Swallowtail Jig   26
22. Menuet (Petzold)   28
23. Arpeggio Games   30
24. Ma Yofus   32

Sprinting Away
25. Terzinka   34
26. Allegretto (Lebrun)   36
27. Early one morning   37
28. Gymnopédie (Satie)   38
29. Gavotta (Vivaldi)   40
30. Celebration Canon   42

Mini Duet Warm-ups

These six short duets explore different cello techniques and skills. Some have an easier part (top), and a harder part (lower). Choose a part to suit and enjoy some fun warm-ups.

Jazzy jogging rhythm

top: short bow strokes, middle of the bow; *lower*: 2nd and 3rd fingers

Arpeggio workout

both parts: G major, D major, and A minor arpeggios

swap parts on repeat

Scale the heights

top: descending G major scale; *lower*: 1st and 4th positions

'Jazzy jogging rhythm' and 'Scale the heights' © Oxford University Press 2023 and 2025. 'Arpeggio workout' © Oxford University Press 2025. Photocopying this copyright material is ILLEGAL.

Smooth talking

both parts: legato playing, two-note slurs, 2nd and 3rd fingers

Moving back

both parts: backward extensions, B♭ major scale, 2nd fingers and slurs

swap parts on repeat

Moving forward

top part: forward extensions, 4th position; *lower*: forward extensions and ostinato

1. Let's Celebrate!

KB & DB

2. Bird Song

KB & DB

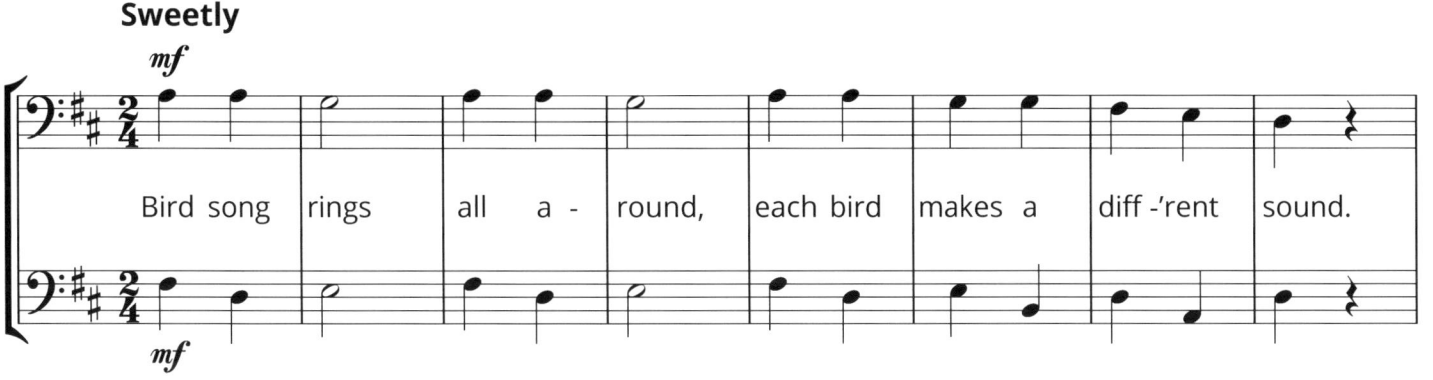

Bird song rings all a - round, each bird makes a diff -'rent sound.

Cuc - koo, cuc - koo, hear the song, lis - ten and we'll play a - long.

Black - bird with his bead - y eye, whi - stles to the morn - ing sky,

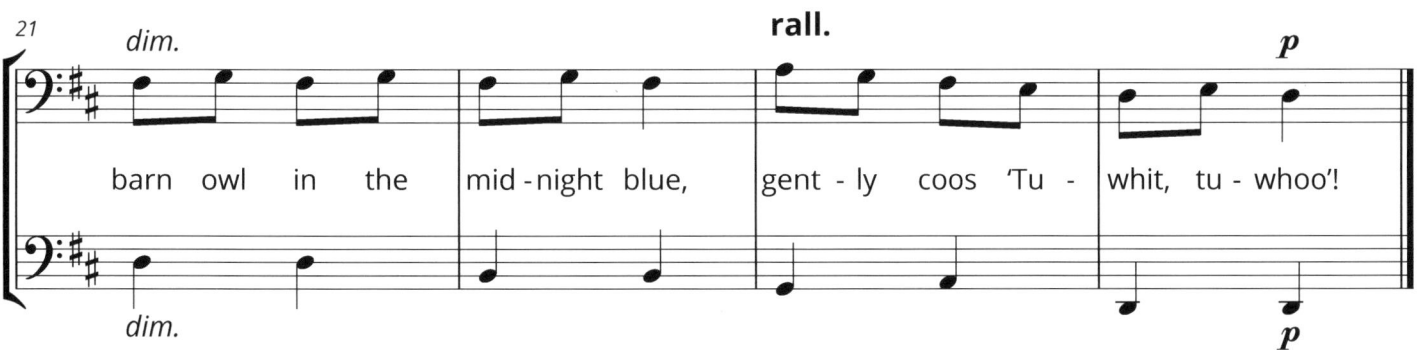

barn owl in the mid - night blue, gent - ly coos 'Tu - whit, tu - whoo'!

3. Run for your life!

KB & DB

With excitement

accel.

4. Bill Grogan's Goat

Echo Song

American folk tune
arr. KB & DB

With a smile!

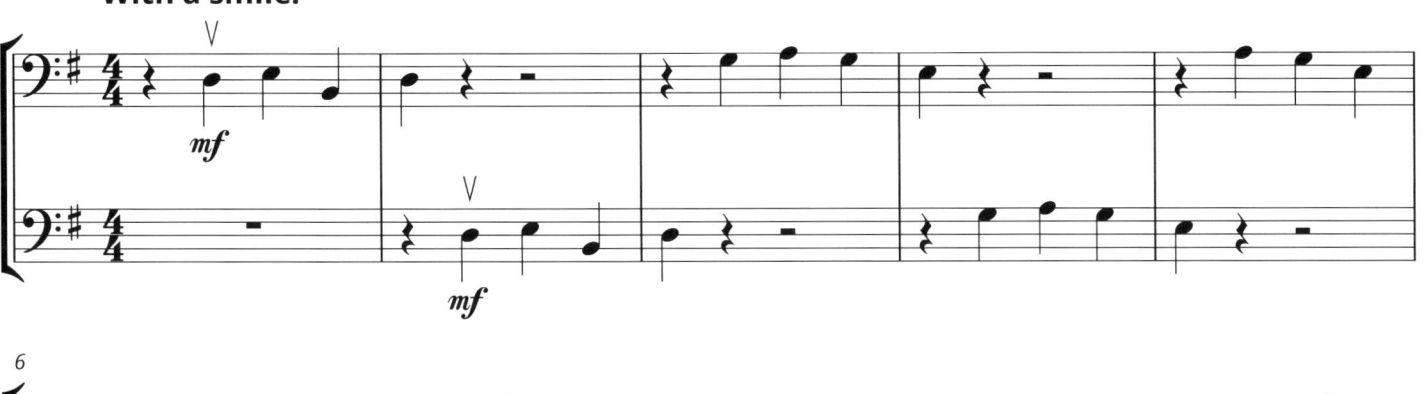

Optional 3rd part *

With a smile!

* This piece can be played as a duet, with the two parts echoing eath other, or as a trio, adding the optional 3rd part.

5. Lani sem kupil

Last year I bought

Slovenian folk tune
arr. KB & DB

This song is about greedy people who always want more, no matter how many presents they're given.

6. Silver Moon Boat

Xiao Yin Chuan

Chinese folk tune
arr. KB & DB

Gently rocking

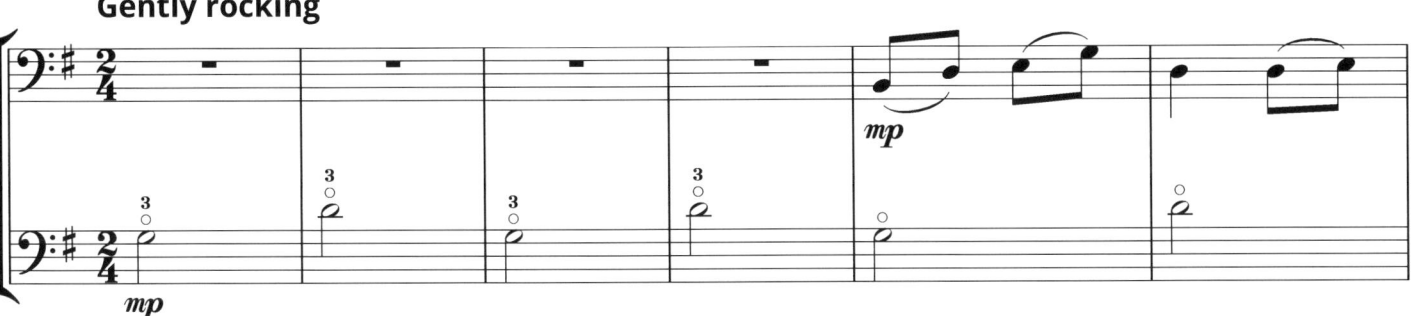

slower

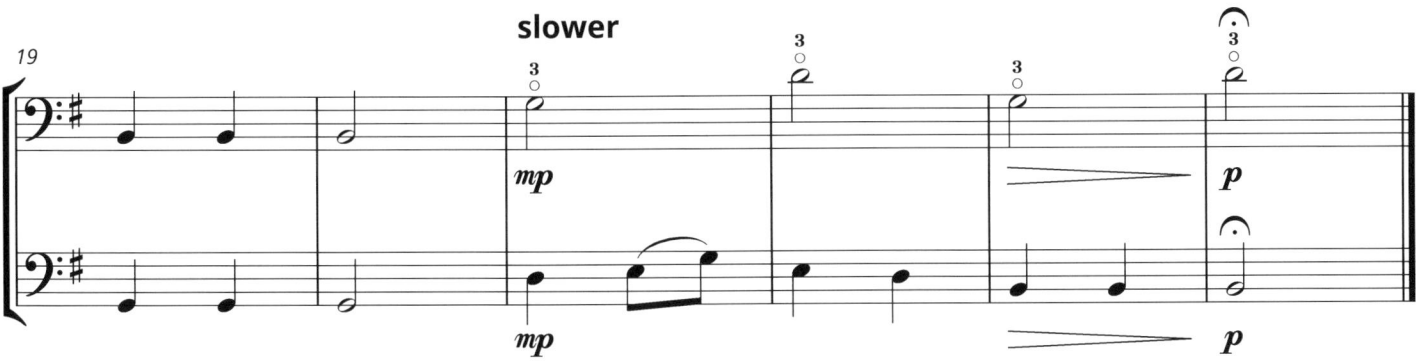

7. Buttered Peas

Pwt ar y Bys

Welsh folk tune
arr. KB & DB

Swap parts on the repeats.

8. Sharing a Surprise!

from Symphony No. 94 (*The Surprise*)

Joseph Haydn (1732–1809)
arr. KB & DB

Allegretto

9. Lullaby for Angus

KB & DB

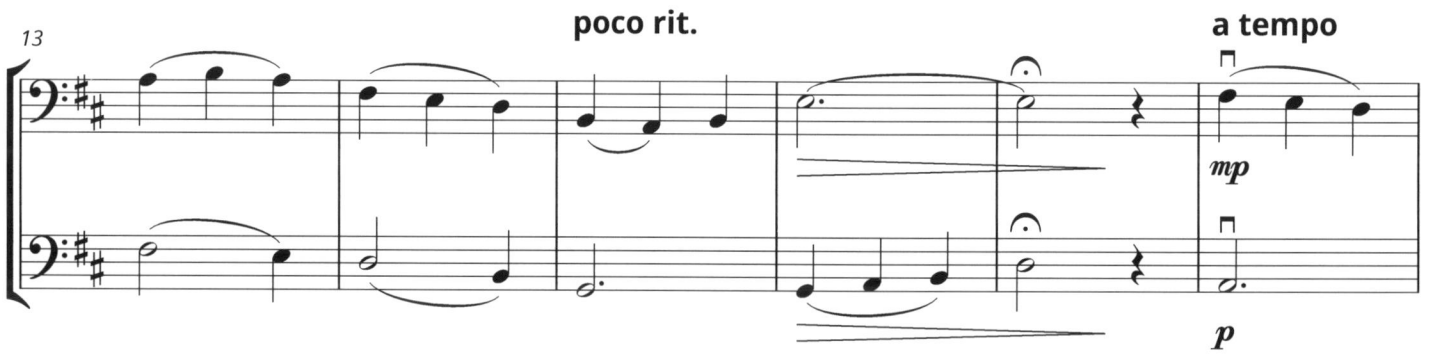

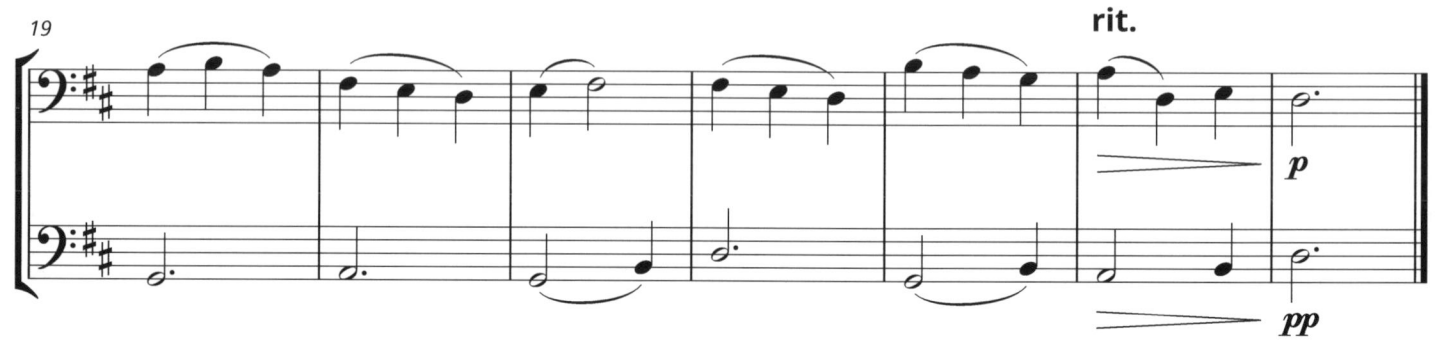

10. Two Trick Pony

American folk tune
arr. KB & DB

11. Sort of Rocky

KB & DB

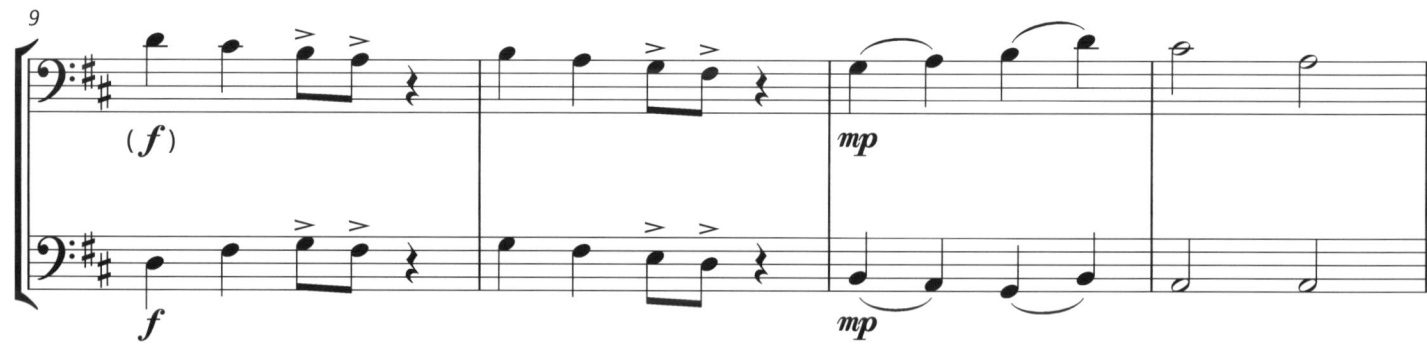

12. Eh soom boo kawaya

Nigerian folk tune
arr. KB & DB

This folk song, traditional to the Ibibio people of Nigeria, loosely translates as: fishermen are out fishing and when it starts to rain they have to paddle faster!

13. Morag's Cradle Song

Scottish folk tune
arr. KB & DB

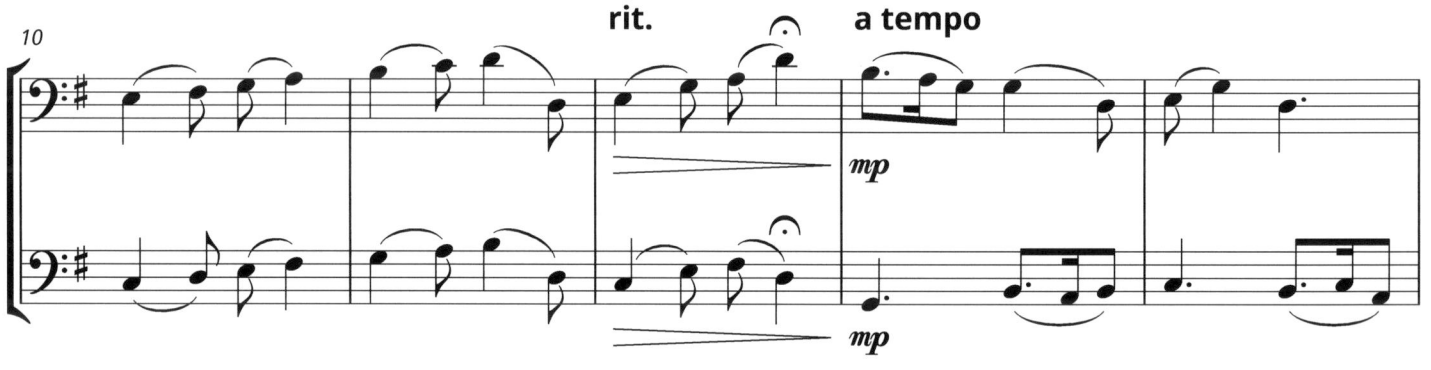

14. Melody

from String Quartet No. 13, Op. 130, 4th movement

Ludwig van Beethoven (1770–1827)

arr. KB & DB

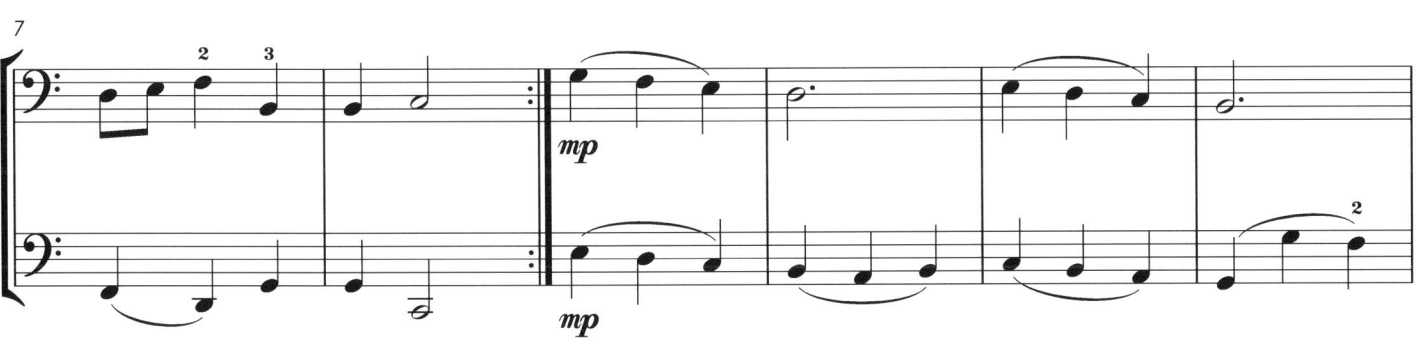

15. Rondeau

from String Quartet, Op. 1 No. 6

Joseph Bologne, Chevalier de Saint-Georges (1745–99)

arr. KB & DB

16. March

No. 3 from *Six Marches*, HWV419

George Frederick Handel (1685–1759)
arr. KB & DB

17. Simple Gifts

Joseph Brackett (1797–1882)
arr. KB & DB

18. One, two, three, four, paper hat

Een, twee, drie, vier, hoedje van papier

Dutch folk tune
arr. KB & DB

19. Dance

adapted from 12 German Dances, WoO 13 No. 9

Ludwig van Beethoven (1770–1827)
arr. KB & DB

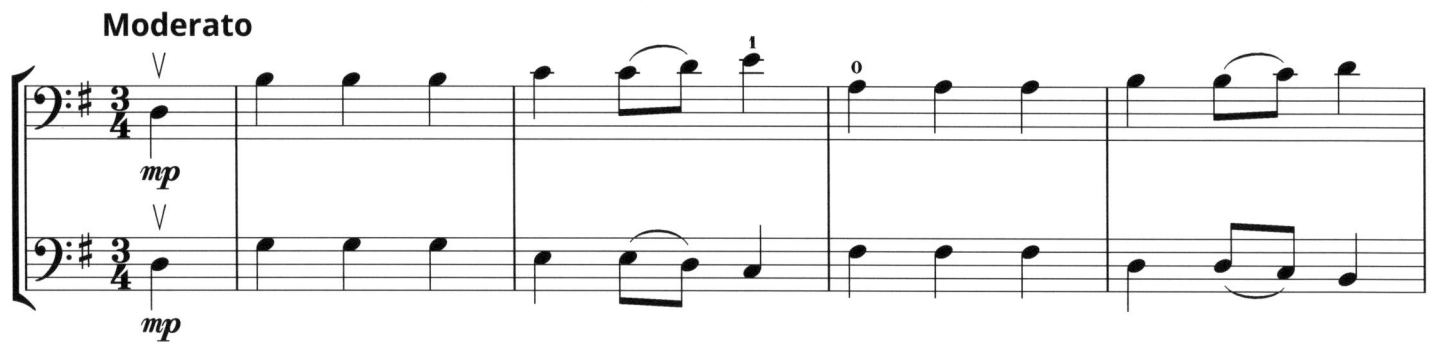

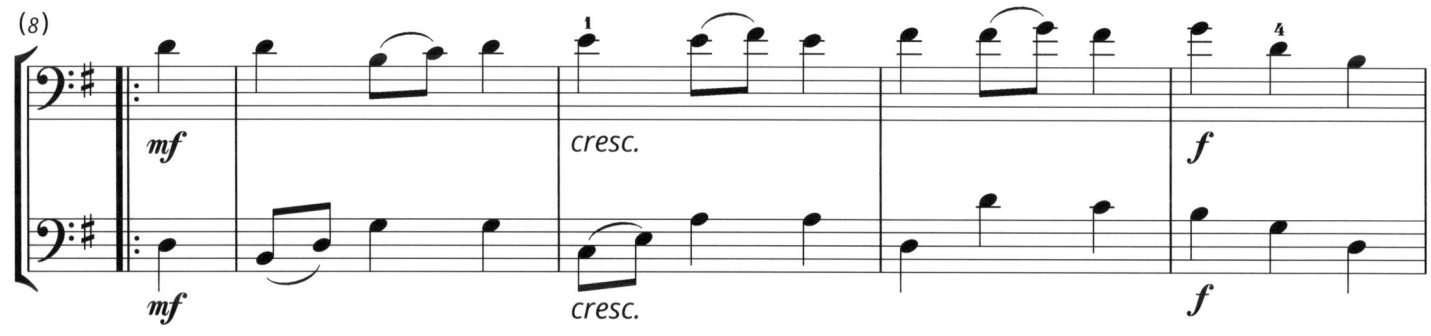

Swap parts on the repeats.

20. La Mourisque

Tylman Susato (*c.*1510/15–*c.*1570)
arr. KB & DB

21. Swallowtail Jig

Irish folk tune
arr. KB & DB

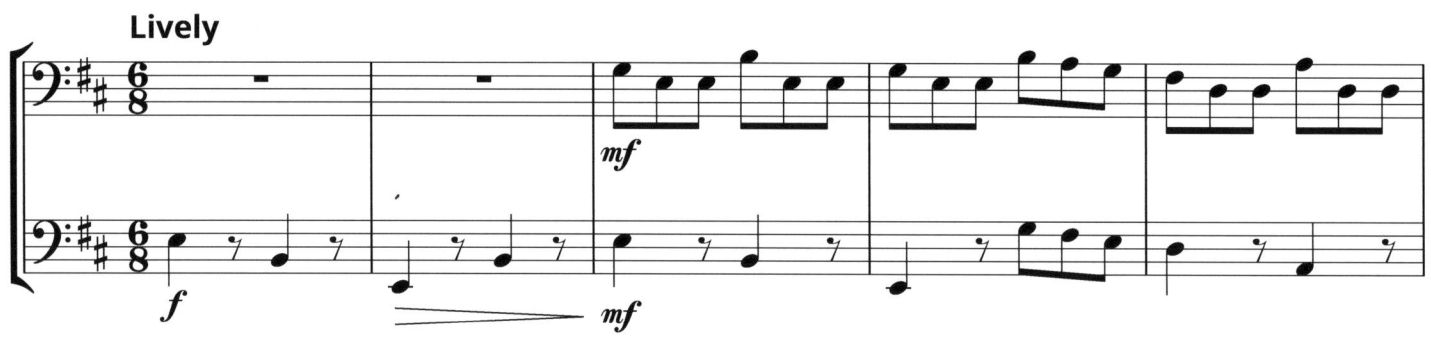

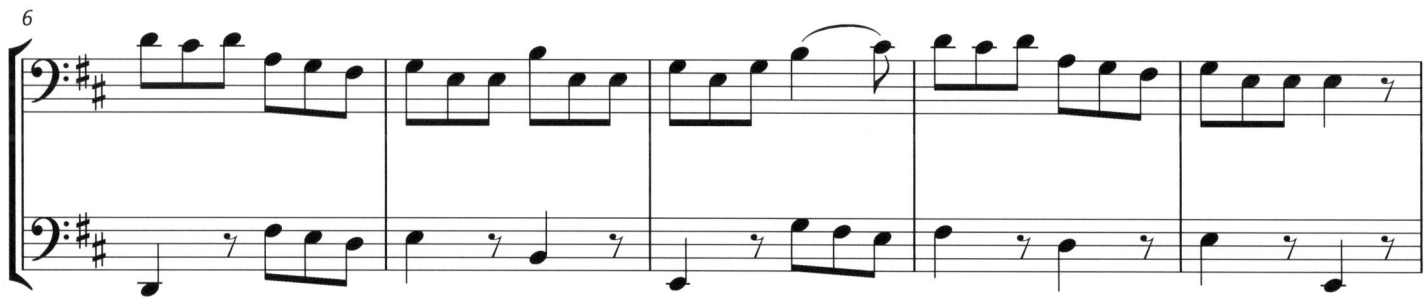

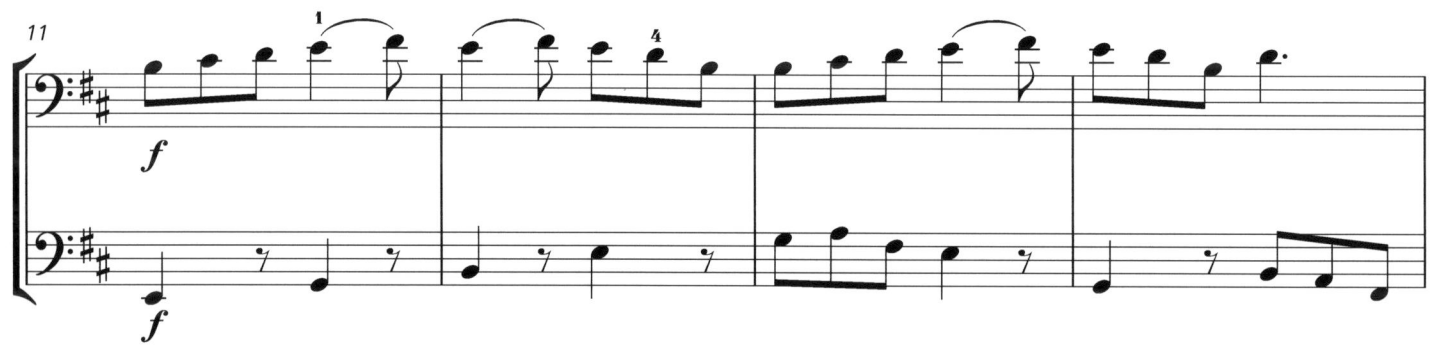

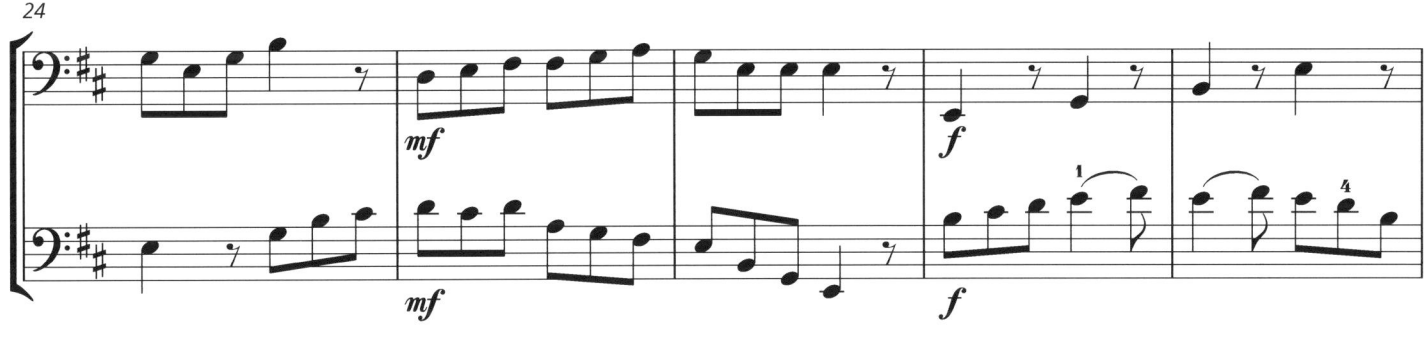

slower · rit. · quick as you can!

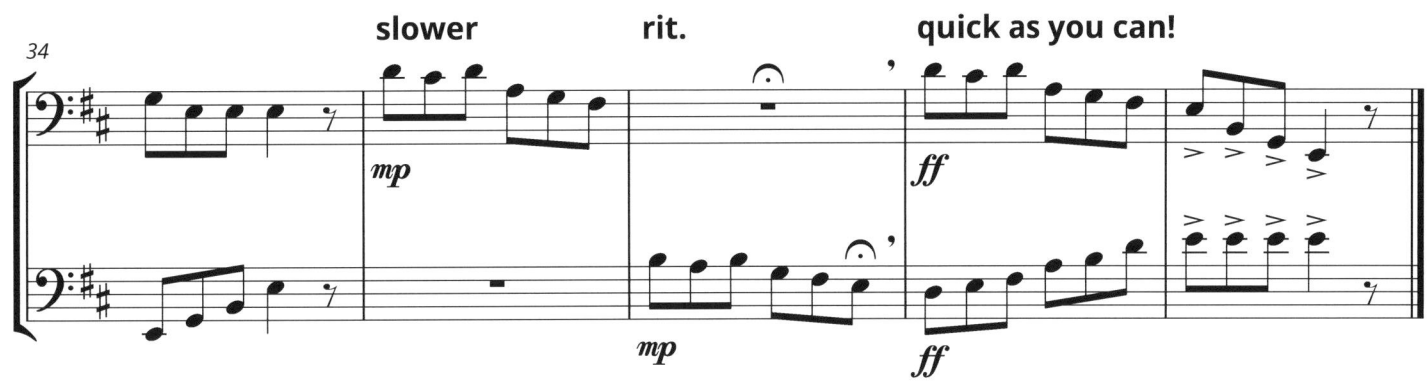

22. Menuet

from *The Anna Magdalena Bach Book of 1725*

Christian Petzold (1677–1733)
arr. KB & DB

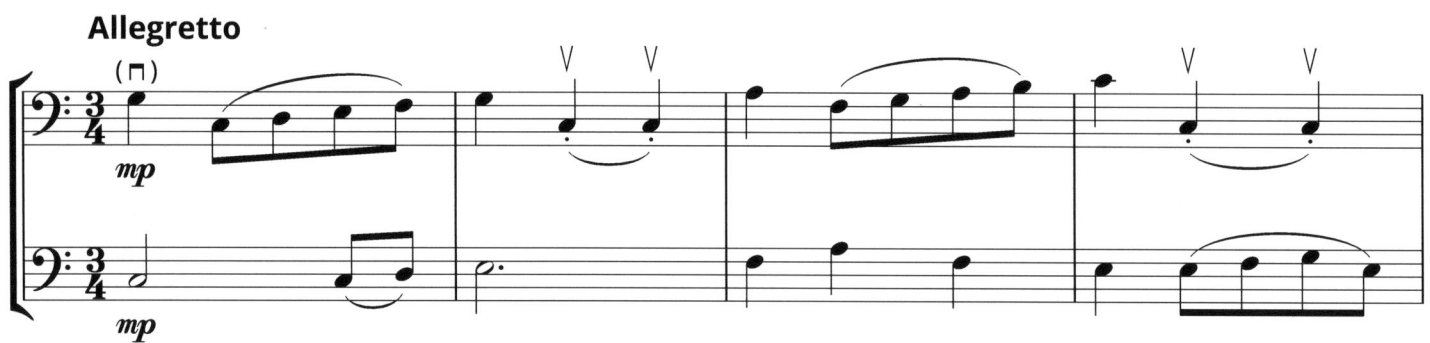

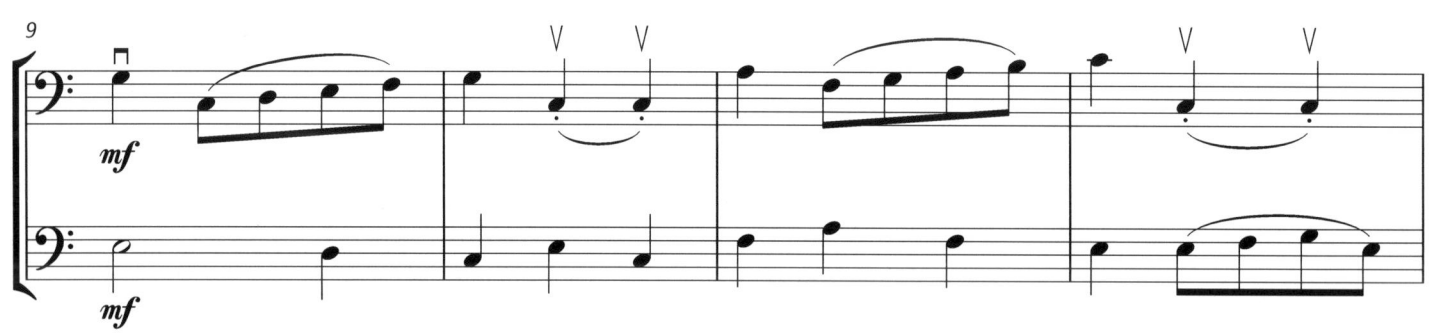

for Angus

23. Arpeggio Games

KB & DB

With energy

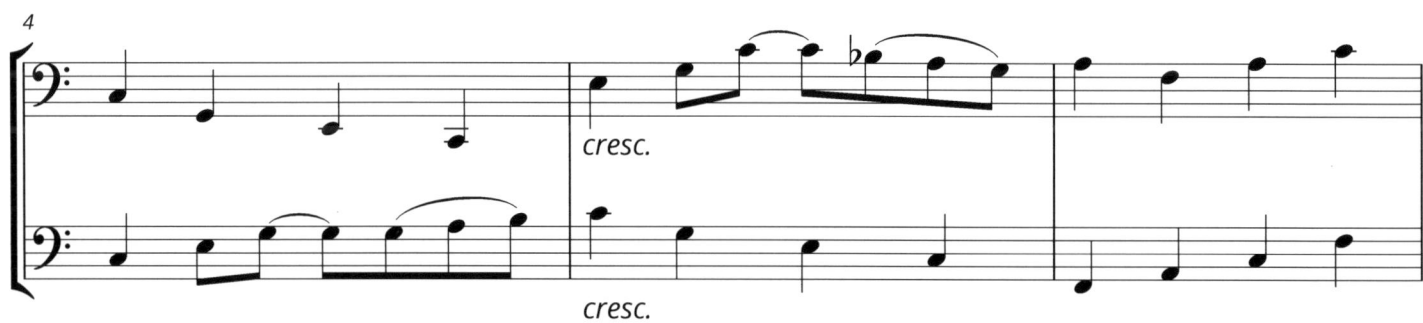

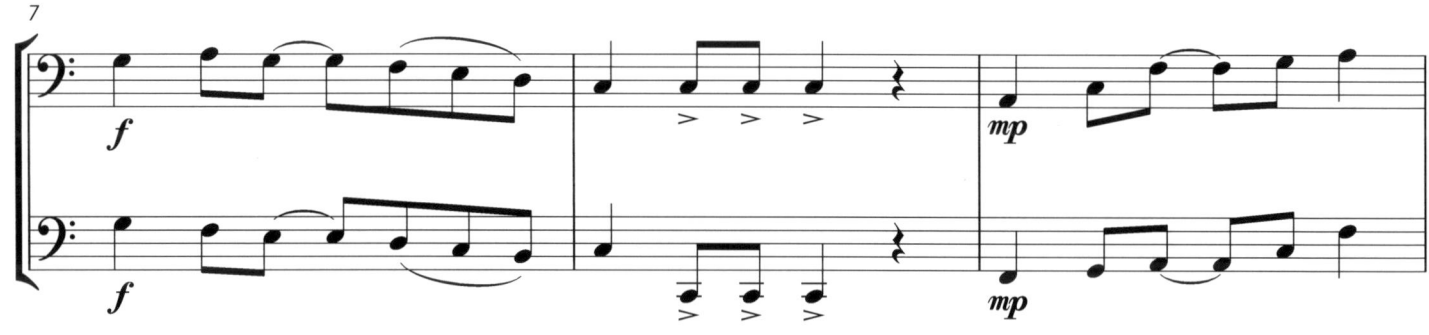

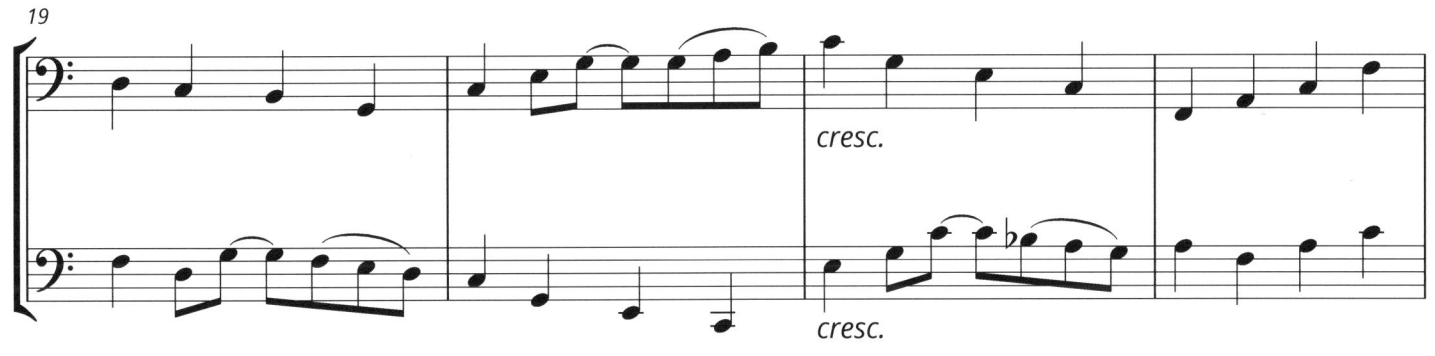

24. Ma Yofus

How Beautiful (also known as *Tanz, Tanz Yidelekh*)

Klezmer folk tune
arr. KB & DB

25. Terzinka

Slovenian folk tune
arr. KB & DB

Allegretto

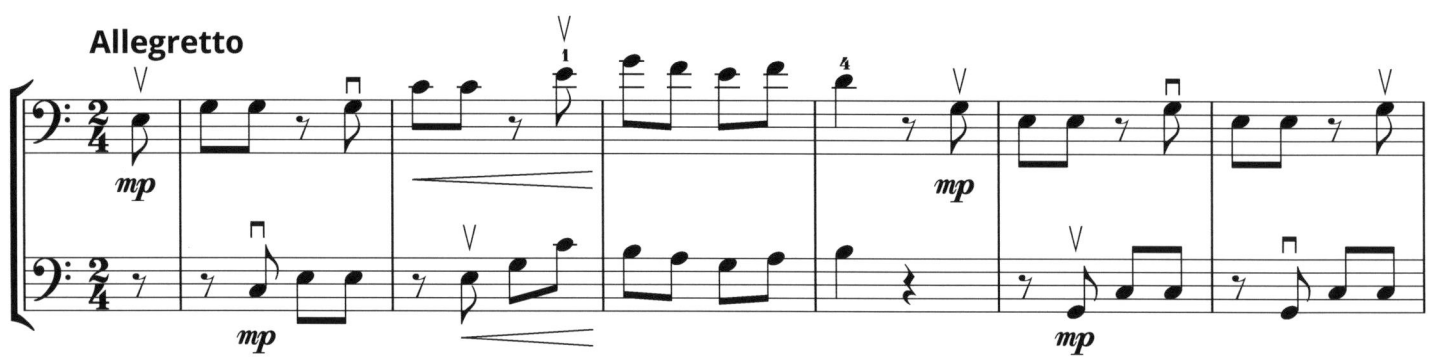

26. Allegretto

from Op. 1 No. 3

Francesca Lebrun (1756–91)
arr. KB & DB

27. Early one morning

English folk tune
arr. KB & DB

28. Gymnopédie

No. 1 of *Trois gymnopédies*

Erik Satie (1866–1925)
arr. KB & DB

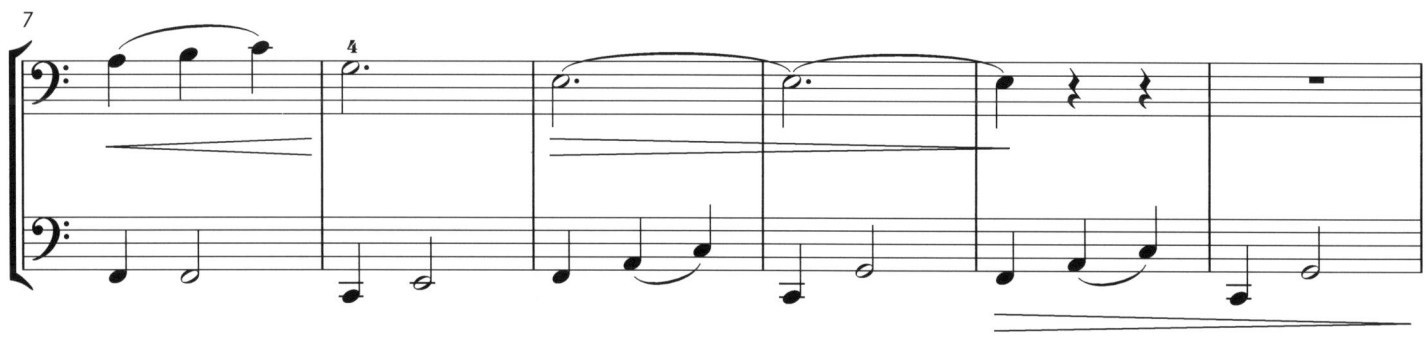

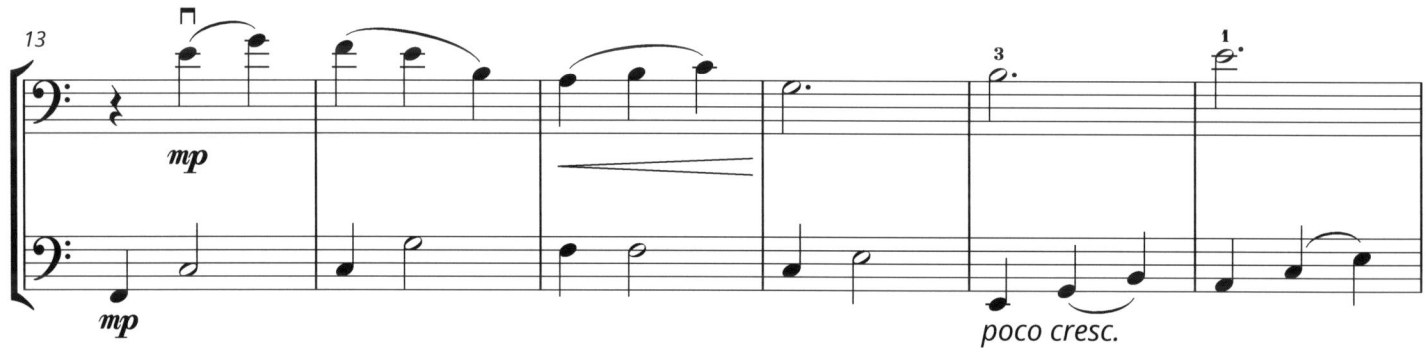

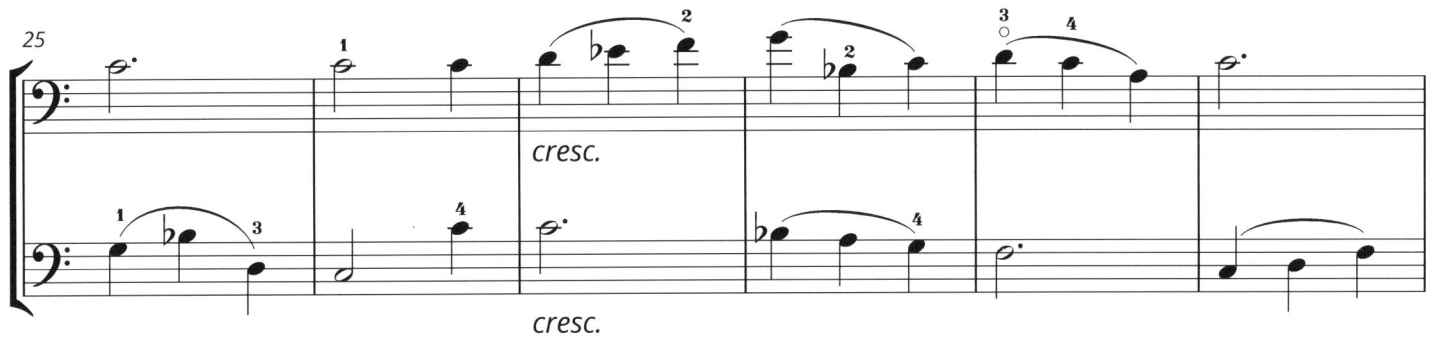

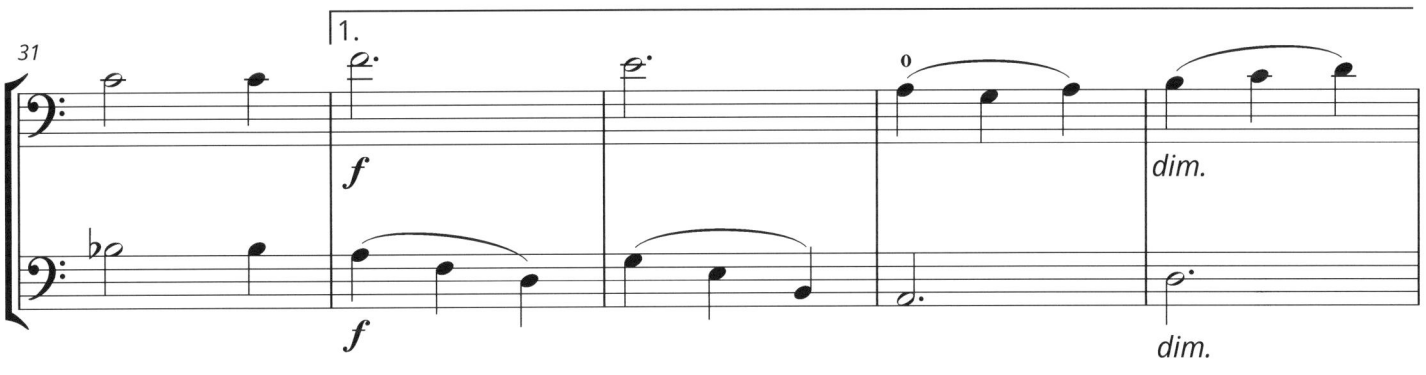

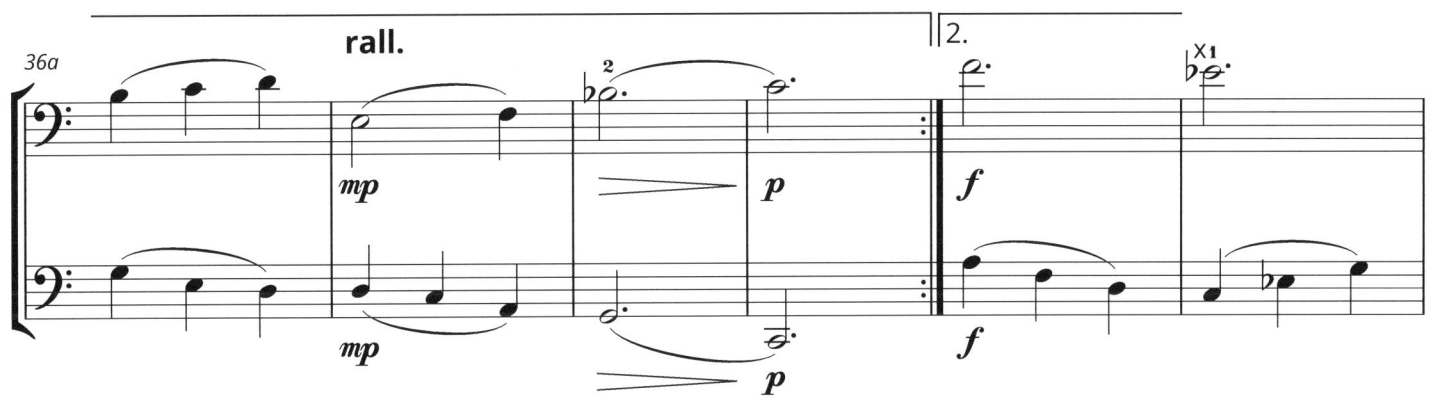

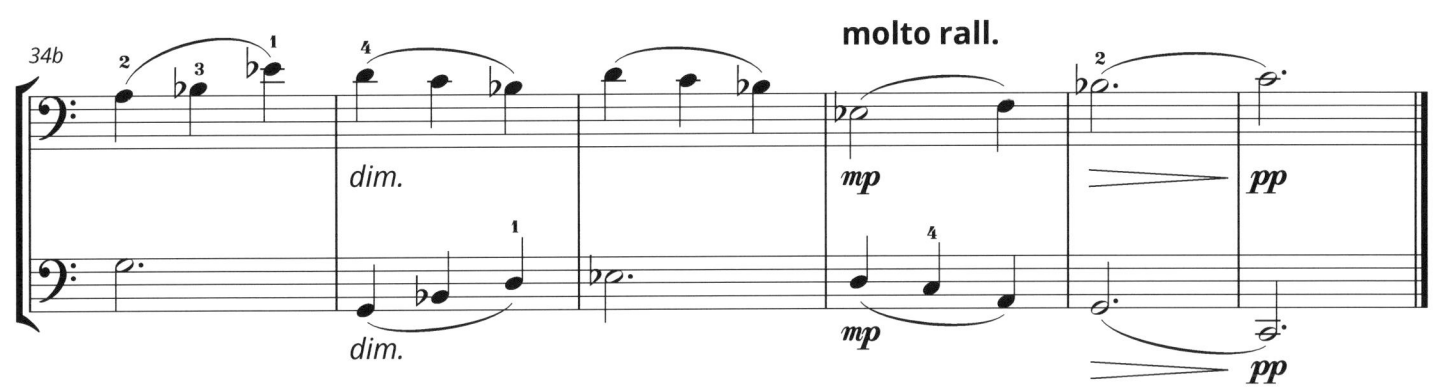

29. Gavotta

from Op. 2 No. 9, RV 16

Antonio Vivaldi (1678–1741)
arr. KB & DB

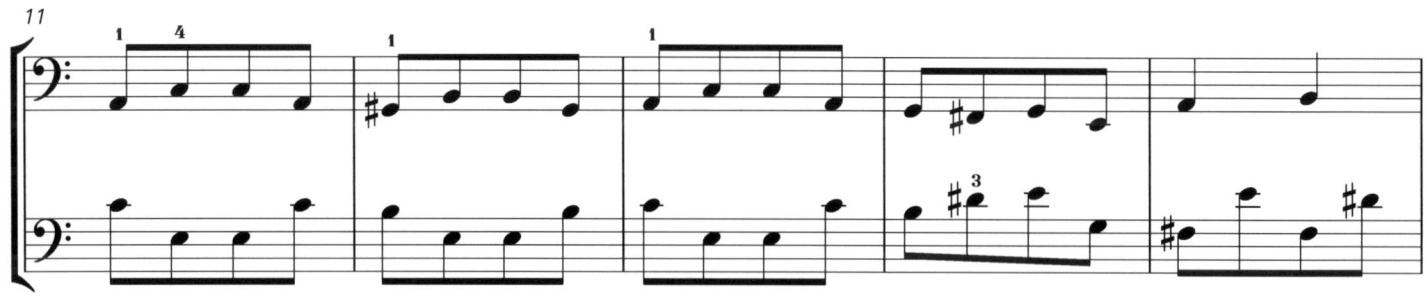

30. Celebration Canon

KB & DB

With a sense of achievement

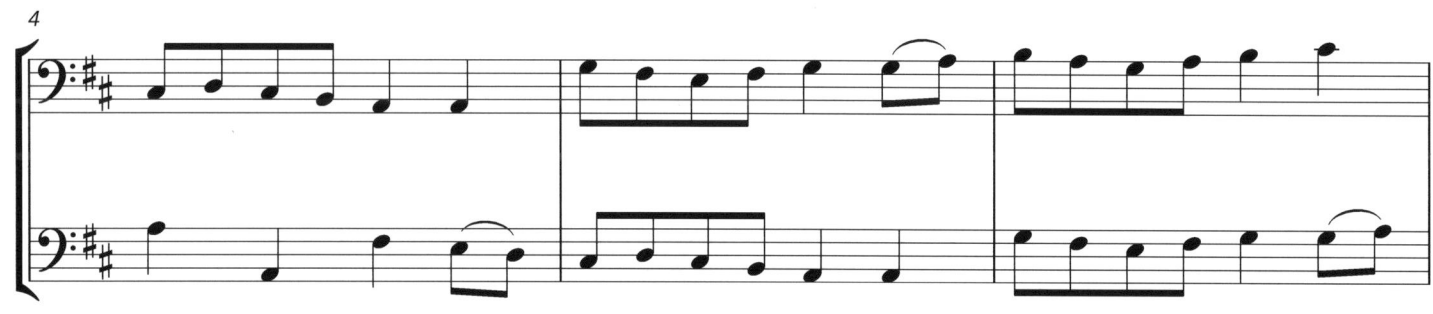